Grace Paull

FRESH EGGS
EGGS
FRESH EGGS
Grace Paull

Grace Paull

Author and Illustrator of Children's Books

Gertrude F. Johns

A Pine Tree Press Publication
North Country Books, Inc.
Utica, New York

Editorial assistance and computer typesetting courtesy of Cynthia F. Bright, Bright Mountain Books, Inc.,
138 Springside Road, Asheville, North Carolina 28803

Printed in the United States of America

ISBN: 0-9629159-7-1

Dedicated to nieces and nephews
of Grace Paull

Arvin Trevvett
Winifred Trevvett Hall
Herbert Trevvett
James Trevvett
Gordon Paull
Elsie Paull Wilcott

Contents

Illustrations

Illustrations (continued)

Preface

My first acquaintance with Grace Paull was while teaching fourth grade at Poland Central School in Poland, New York. I remember taking my students to her studio on the hill in nearby Cold Brook. Little did I realize that some day I would be writing about her accomplishments.

What an interesting life she led! Since I began writing her biography, I have made contact with many of her friends as well as her nieces and nephews. Each one has made a contribution to this book. Much of the information has come from articles in the *Utica Observer-Dispatch* and the *Herkimer Evening Telegram* provided by family members.

Special thanks are due to Grace's relatives and friends who lent me photographs or shared their memories of her: Susan McVoy Barnard, Henry Blue, Fred Coonradt, Tom Gates, Winifred Trevvett Hall, Paula Johnson, Frances Kubick, Mary Kubick, Gordon Paull, Carla Pogonowski, Nancy Coonradt Rickard, Doris and Herbert Trevvett, and Frances Warren.

I sincerely hope that you will get as much enjoyment out of reading this book as I have enjoyed writing it.

—Gertrude F. Johns
April 1994

Grace Paull at work in her studio.

Grace Paull

Arvin and Hannah Paull, Grace's father and mother.

Grace, Sara, and Theodore Paull, about 1906.

1. Early Years and Accomplishments

Grace, the daughter of Hannah and Arvin Paull, was born October 7, 1898, on the farm that had been in her mother's family for four generations. The farm was located just outside the village of Cold Brook, New York, in the foothills of the Adirondack Mountains, surrounded by hills and valleys. For miles one could see the green foliage in the summer, the colorful maple trees in autumn, and the snow-covered ground in winter.

Grace had a sister Sara and a brother Theodore. As children, they lived in Utica and Lyons Falls, New York, and in a number of New England towns where their father's work in the paper manufacturing industry took him. For a time the family lived in Montreal and then returned to Utica.

Grace's high school course begun in Montreal was completed at Utica Free Academy. There the artist-to-be tackled every possible art course taught by Miss Mabel E. Northrup who, through

Grace as a high school graduate.

the years, encouraged a number of now famous artists.

After taking a three-year general arts course at Pratt Institute, Grace continued her studies at the Art Students' League and the Grand Central Art School. One of her first jobs was working for a New York City manufacturing concern doing lettering and drawing.

A group of Grace's classmates at Pratt Institute.

In the 1920s, she was employed by Norcross Greeting Cards, painting cards on an assembly line. She worked for Norcross for twenty-five to thirty years, eventually designing all-occasion cards, Valentines, Christmas cards, seals, tags, and wrapping paper. For a time during the Depression, Grace was laid off from Norcross and returned home to work as a substitute teacher.

Tom Gates of Barneveld, New York, has a collection of Norcross cards designed by Miss Paull. Tom's uncle had a store in the '30s, '40s,

Giftwrap designed by Grace Paull for Norcross.

and '50s, where he sold the Norcross cards, and Tom acquired them from his uncle's estate. They are unique. Many of the Christmas cards are stand-up cards and many have inserts. One stand-up Christmas card is of Santa Claus made so that the little girl sitting on his lap is an insert. Upon removing the insert you will find a message inside.

In addition to greeting cards, Grace designed giftwrap paper and tags. One of the name tags is Santa playing a grand piano. This can be folded to look like a real piano. How clever and talented she was!

Pictured on the next several pages are cards from Tom's collection. The card which depicts a house front is a stand-up card. The doorway has a wreath on it with a big red bow. Beside it, in the window, is an insert. Two little birds hold a songbook in their wings. The caption inside reads, "These little bluebirds sing a song, Merry Christmas all day long." Another insert in the upstairs window is a little kitten. The insert reads, "This little kitten comes to greet, Someone very dear and sweet."

While working with Norcross Greeting Cards, Grace realized that what she really wanted to do was to illustrate children's books. It just happened that her office was in the same building with Doubleday, Doran and Company. One day Grace finally summoned up enough courage to go to see them. She took some samples of her drawings with her. The editor of junior books looked at the samples and gave her a book to illustrate,

FOR A
Darling
Granddaughter

TO HELP YOU GET BETTER
A WISHING WELL

TO MY
UNCLE

Feeling
Better?
GOOD!

HAPPY BIRTHDAY

a children's book written by Margery Williams Bianco, a well-known children's author. How thrilled she was when the first book she illustrated was published!

Miss Paull used many different mediums in her artwork. She was most famous for her lithography, a process in which the image was drawn on a flat stone with a greasy material to which the printing ink would adhere. After printing from the stone, it could be cleaned and reused. Her lithographs were used on postcards, writing paper, book covers, and Christmas cards, as well as in books.

As her reputation grew, she illustrated books on a freelance basis for several different publishers, among them Doubleday & Company, Viking Press, Thomas Y. Crowell, Frederick Stokes, and Macmillan Company. Usually she would be given the manuscript along with the specifications as to size, number of colors, type of reproduction, and budget. She planned the book's illustrations, with a final approval by the editor.

When she began working on the illustrations for *Rowena Carey* by Ruth Langland Holberg, she was sent by Doubleday to Rockport, Massachusetts, to acquaint herself with the terrain since the story was about a girl who actually lived in that New England town.

Creating an illustration through lithography.

An author whose stories she illustrated was Clyde Robert Bulla. Mr. Bulla lived on the West

Lithograph of Russian Union Church, drawn by Miss Paull in 1933.

Coast and wrote a series of westerns. Each year Grace would produce the pictures for his latest book. Both the publisher and the author were more than satisfied with the western atmosphere which Miss Paull created with her eastern ponies and her own mental picture of what the Bulla characters should look like.

Grace collaborated with Mr. Bulla on *Surprise for a Cowboy* in 1950. Upon seeing the completed book, he wrote to express his appreciation for her artwork:

> I hope you have seen *Surprise for a Cowboy* by now. Miss Riley sent me copies that arrived last week, and I thought the pictures reproduced beautifully. I'm still trying to decide on my favorite, but they're really all favorites, I like them so much.

Her pen-and-ink drawings were used to illustrate a teenage mystery story, *The Seven and Sam,* written by Mary Urmston of California and published by Doubleday & Company. Another book in which she used this type of illustration is *Lulu's Window,* published by Thomas Y. Crowell Company.

Later on she began to write stories as well as illustrate them. Many of her stories depicted her experiences as a child and contained many scenes

A pen-and-ink drawing for *The Seven and Sam*, published by Doubleday in 1955.

familiar to the Cold Brook area—sleigh rides, the making of maple sugar, sliding down hill, a picnic in the woods, horseback riding.

Come to the City told about things to see in New York City. It showed people climbing the stairs to the top of the Statue of Liberty, and it told about the many things to be seen from there, like the ships in the harbor, the many streets, and the tall buildings.

One memorable book, *Pancakes for Breakfast*, showed how maple syrup was made. There was

Illustration from *Come to the City,* published by Abelard-Schuman in 1959

a sugar bush not far from her home. The pictures show how they tapped the trees, collected the sap in pails, and boiled the sap in a big iron kettle. The book ended with the children having pancakes for breakfast.

Tom Gates also has a collection of Grace Paull's pictures and illustrations. Among them are:

– a crayon drawing found in the book *Pioneer Art in America,*

– a lithograph from *Uncle Sam's Story Book,*

– a pen and ink drawing from *Teeny and the Tall Man,*

– a crayon drawing of "The Blizzard" from *Winter on the Prairie,*

– "Come On, Stupid" - original drawing from *Betsy and the Proud House,*

– the little boy picture of Herbie Trevvett found in the book *A Horse to Ride.*

While living on Washington Square in New York City, Miss Paull did a lithograph of the square which was later purchased by the Congressional Library in Washington. Eleanor Roosevelt was pictured in that lithograph.

Winifred Trevvett reading *Pancakes for Breakfast.*

Plymouth Congregational Church on Oneida Square and Church of St. John, Utica, New York.

2. The Studio

Although Grace worked at her studio in New York City during the winter months, she always would come back to the Cold Brook farm in the summertime to be near her family and friends. She would come north in June and stay at least until the first snowfall.

One winter she stayed in Utica and worked in a studio on State Street. There she made a number of sketches of historic places in and around Utica. These included lithographs of such Utica landmarks as Grace Church, Oneida Square, Plymouth Congregational Church, and the Church of St. John's, and other area places of historical interest such as General Herkimer's Homestead, Fort Herkimer Church, Baron Von Steuben's House, and, of course, the old flour mill in Cold Brook. These works have been exhibited throughout New York State and appeared on postcards that were sold in Utica and surrounding areas.

The architecture of the many beautiful homes, churches, and buildings in the area that were built in the eighteenth and nineteenth centuries

Old Fort Herkimer Church, south of Herkimer, New York.

were of special interest to Miss Paull. People would ask her to sketch or paint a favorite place or a particular scene, and many local residents commissioned paintings of their own homes. At art exhibits throughout the country her lithographs, many of them depicting scenes in and around the Cold Brook area, received high praise.

In 1941, Grace built a studio on the North Country farmland originally owned by Miss Paull's grandfather, Griffith W. Jones. It was designed by a Utica architect, Charles Greenidge, and built by a neighbor, Lyle Carpenter. Later, Grace "built" Lyle's home in her style.

This picture of Lyle Carpenter's house and barn now hangs in Joe and Carla Pogonowski's home.

Inside was a large room called the artist's workroom, with its knotty pine walls, huge stone fireplace, ceiling-high open bookcases, early American furniture, china and glassware, mingled with Mexican pottery and signed prints of contemporary artists. The room was bright and cheerful with the large windows letting in plenty of light. Looking out these windows onto the terrace and the countryside, Grace could see the hills and the valleys, the green grass, and the flowers in bloom in the garden.

The studio on the hill; Grace with Theodore and Jennie.

Behind the studio, in an adjoining field, were two horses owned by Miss Paull. She used them as models in some of her illustrations. Turk, a palomino, was the horse that was illustrated in her book, *A Horse to Ride*.

My daughter Lois, and no doubt many other Poland residents, remembers going to her studio on the hill and seeing a beautiful horse grazing in the pasture next to the studio. It was the same one she had seen in Miss Paull's books at the school library.

Soon after the studio was built, another Poland

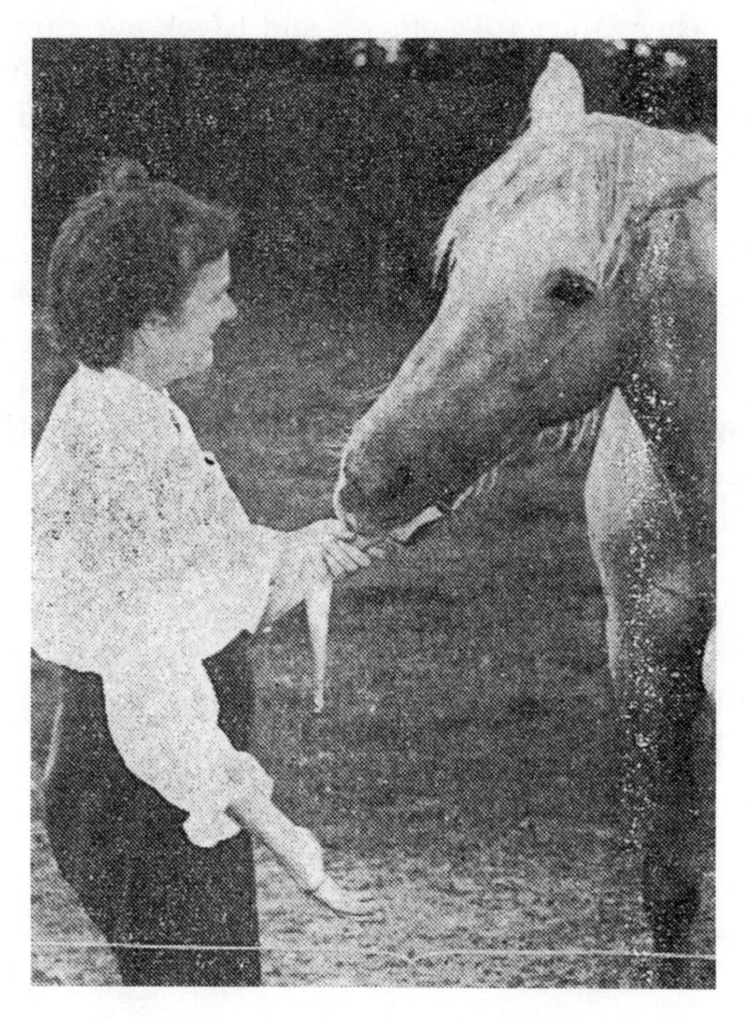

Grace with one of her beautiful Palominos.

teacher, Marietta Lefevre, and I took our third and fourth graders to the studio one afternoon in June. Grace showed us all the steps she went through to make book illustrations.

Many of Miss Paull's books were written for the preschooler. Others she illustrated included ones geared through the teen level. For class projects, teachers often assigned students to write letters to her. "It was a real chore answering all of them," she said, but as with everything she did, the letters were each answered with loving care.

While living in her studio on the hill, many of the children in the area would stop by to see her. She always had cookies and lemonade for them, and they became characters in her books.

Grace at her drawing board.

Helen Sewell and Grace Paull at Pratt Institute.

3. Friends and Relatives

From Tom Gates I learned about a freelance artist from Utica, Margaret Alexander, who was a very dear friend of Grace Paull's. She lived near her in New York City in the 1930s. Margaret was designing greeting cards at the time and also creating art pottery sculptural pieces for Inwood Pottery Studios on 168th Street. Margaret was interested in breaking into children's book illustration. Grace would often visit Margaret to encourage her and to provide suggestions about publishing. Presently, a retrospective show of Margaret's artwork is planned at Munson-Williams-Proctor School of Art in Utica.

A classmate at Pratt Institute, Helen Sewell, became one of Grace's life-long friends. Both designed greeting cards for Norcross and illustrated children's books for many years. Helen and Grace had a mutual friend in Ethel Swantees. In their later years, Ethel lived across the road from Grace in Cold Brook and was an artist noted for her oil paintings. Ethel's oil paintings and Grace Paull's artwork were both exhibited at Fynmore Studios in Boonville, New York.

Just up the street from the old mill lived the Buck family. Dorothy taught high school English at Poland Central School, and Ellsworth was principal of the school for several years. Their three children are Frances, Thomas, and Janice. Janice was Grace's godchild and helped Grace for a while at the Old Feed Mill Gallery.

In Fran Kubick's home hangs a picture of Lewey Lake near Speculator. One day in summer, the Buck family had invited Grace to go with them to Lewey Lake for a picnic. To show her gratitude, she painted a beautiful picture for them.

The house in which Fran grew up in Poland was painted as a wedding present for Fran and Matt Kubick by "Aunt Grace." She painted it in 1956, when she spent the winter in Cold Brook with Lena Newberry.

Fran's daughter, Mary Kubick, was a reporter for *The Evening Telegram* in Herkimer for a few years. Mary wrote a feature article for the paper that was published January 26, 1989, soon after Grace's ninetieth birthday. Mary's most vivid memory as a child going into the gallery is of the smell of soaps and candles and the rich timber of the mill. Janice's home also contains several of Grace's lithographs and paintings.

Two of "Aunt Grace's" pictures in Frances Kubick's home are of the Buck homestead and Lewey Lake.

On Route 8, about an hour's drive north of Cold Brook, there is a beautiful lake called Piseco. Grace had several friends who had camps on this lake. One of these camps belonged to the Coonradt family. Grace and her sister Sara often went to this camp to visit their friend Mattie. The picture of Piseco Lake was painted by Grace Paull for Mattie about forty years ago and now belongs to Mattie's grandson Fred Coonradt.

Elon Coonradt, Mattie's son, worked for many years at Commercial Travelers, an insurance company owned by the Trevvetts. Elon's wife

Piseco Lake

Louise was a very dear friend of Sara and Grace's. I remember an occasion at Dorcas meeting when Louise, Grace, and Sara were on the committee to serve refreshments after the meeting. What a surprise we had when we came out of the meeting room to find that our refreshments that night consisted of "Jackwax"—maple syrup on fresh fallen snow!

Grace's sister Sara also attended Pratt Institute. She married Edward Trevvett and they had four children: Arvin, Winifred, Herbert, and James. Her brother Theodore and his wife Jennie were the parents of Gordon and Elsie. These were the nieces and nephews Grace frequently used as models for her children's books. Both families lived in the Cold Brook farmhouse.

Winifred Trevvett Hall shared with me many of her memories of her Aunt Grace, especially of the holidays. Christmas was Grace's favorite. Winifred told me that they always received some unique gift from her—a keepsake that they could cherish forever.

Winifred remembers that Grace loved to go on picnics with the family. The West Canada Creek flowed for miles through the countryside, winding its way through villages and towns and finally dumping its waters into the Mohawk River at Herkimer. There were waterfalls along its

Elsie, Gordon, and Theodore bringing home the tree.

course, and in the '20s and '30s several covered bridges spanned the creek. Grace carried her easel, charcoal, pencils, and other art supplies with her, and after eating a hearty picnic lunch, would sit down and paint. Often she would be

Christmas at the homestead about 1950: Gordon Paull, Herbie Trevvett standing in background, James Trevvett with Grace's kitten Chippie, Winifred T. Hall, Grace Paull, James Wilcott, Elsie Paull Wilcott, Jennie and Theodore Paull, Sara Trevvett, Grace's dog Patsy in foreground.

seen by the roadside sketching her pictures.

Grace's book *Come to the Country* reveals how much she enjoyed every aspect of nature as she walked through the woods. On each page was one caption. The pictures told the rest of the story—every little detail of what she saw and how she felt as she walked through the woods. The children loved the stories and learned a lot from them.

While spending one winter with her Aunt Sara and Uncle Guy Shorey at Gorham, a place located high in the White Mountains of New Hampshire, Grace wrote *Snowed-in Hill.* It is a true story about life in this mountainous region in winter, and her illustrations were scenes from the area surrounding her. The father and mother in the book were Theodore and Jennie Paull, the children were Gordon and Elsie, and the other lady depicted in the story was Sylvia Horne, postmistress of Cold Brook at the time the book was written.

Uncle Guy owned a drugstore in Gorham, New Hampshire, which was also his professional photography studio. Previous to this time he had owned the Mt. Crescent House at Randolph, New Hampshire. His daughter, Gwen, and her husband Jack Boothman, ran the Mt. Crescent House for awhile, but the hotel burned a few

Uncle Guy, Aunt Sara, and Gwen Shorey
in Gorham, New Hampshire.

years ago, and the Boothmans now run a large farm called Cold Brook Farms. They have three children—Becky, Sally, and Susan.

Sign in front of the Old Feed Mill Gallery
made by Henry Blue.

4. The Yellow House and The Old Feed Mill Gallery

In 1954, Miss Paull bought the big yellow house in the village of Cold Brook and the old flour mill that stood beside it. The mill was built in 1858 and it still stands on the banks of the Cold Brook Stream.

Grace continued to spend her summers in Cold Brook but still spent the winters elsewhere, often in New York where she arranged for projects to be worked on during her summers in the country. Finally, in 1965, she made Cold Brook her permanent year-round home.

During the '50s, Grace began to work more extensively with watercolors and oils and the demand for her pictures grew. Grace had read a book on how to be a successful watercolorist, and it said in order to sell paintings, they needed to be exposed to the public. With that in mind, she converted the old flour mill into an art gallery where her pictures and books could be displayed and sold. As was explained in an article in the *Utica Observer-Dispatch* of November 29, 1961, written by Lyn Simon:

> The mill gallery just happened. It came with the house, and at first, was used simply as a salesroom for her own paintings and other works of art. Eventually it began to include handmade gift items of all descriptions from the area, and now has expanded to take on some imported items, mostly Scandinavian.

These items were purchased each spring in New York City by a friend, Miss Dorothy Voorhees of Brooklyn, a retired librarian who spent each summer in Cold Brook assisting Miss Paull in the operation of the gallery.

Winifred Hall's daughter Sandra helped Grace at the art gallery one summer and enjoyed working there. Many people stopped to shop at the Old Feed Mill Gallery—people from all over the country who would be traveling through to the camps and resort areas in the Adirondacks and neighbors and friends from the area.

Visitors, especially out-of-state ones, often remarked on its old but still intact architecture. The mill contains most of the original equipment, and men especially were intrigued by the maze of cogs, wheels, and belts that once was the heart of the old mill. Everyone loved the

Grace at the Old Feed Mill Gallery.

waterwheel operating at the back of the mill, just below the point where a dam once existed.

The two floors, when Grace owned it, were filled with paintings, books, greeting cards, stationery, antiques, dishes, postcards, and bookmarks. Each and every nook and cranny was filled.

Miss Paull's aunt, Elizabeth C. Jones, also known as Aunt Lizzie, wrote the following poem about Grace and the Old Feed Mill Gallery. It was included in the Cold Brook Centennial Book, published in 1976.

THE OLD FEED MILL
Miss Grace Paull
Artist and Illustrator

Nestled in a pleasant valley
Bordered by a wooded hill,
Stands an unimposing structure
That was once a Grinding Mill.

'Twas a meeting place for farmers
As they brought their home-grown grain,
And a chat in neighborly fashion
Was prolonged on a day of rain.

Many years have passed since those days
When water wheels were the power,
And the wheat and rye and barley
Became in time a household flour.

Later as new methods came in practice
And electricity was installed,
Fewer home-grown crops were planted
And Western grains by rail were hauled.

It was then this thriving Grist Mill
(Now forever past its prime),
That the rumbling of machinery
Was silenced by the changing time.

With an urge to own a gallery
To display the products of her skill,
Was the thought of a local artist
To re-open The Old Feed Mill.

Dust and cobwebs of long standing
Festooned each grinder, window, door,
And the pigeons that had nested
Occupied the upper floor.

Quite undaunted by the labor
This determined artist set about
To remove the worthless rubbish
So in record time it was cleared out.

There is yet some old equipment
One can gaze upon at will,
Which is of the utmost interest
To the guests of The Old Feed Mill.

Lithographs and water-colors
Of the beautiful country-side,
Hang upon the sturdy timbers
And each taste is gratified.

Children's Books, which she's the Author,
and the Illustrator too,
Attract the younger generation
As they pause to look them through.

Christmas cards with simple greetings
Note paper of the same design,
Also Post Cards that picture land marks
Are found within this pleasing shrine.

Some hand-weaving and wood-carving
Crocheted rugs and table mats,
Stenciled towels of many patterns
And fancy bags with matching hats.

There is a showing of Ceramics
To please those who are in line,
For a decorative or useful trinket
Of a quaint or modern design.

And a few antiques remind one
Of the things used years ago,
That have long since been discarded
As every modern home can show.

When each year the Mill is opened
New attractions meet the eye,
And the now increasing business
Requires a partner to stand by.

On display is hand-made jewelry
Deftly created and designed,
By this most capable assistant
Who has the people's taste in mind.

Grace's books and artwork were displayed alongside gifts at the mill gallery.

Earrings, necklaces, pins and bracelets,
Made of silver with copper wire,
Or on copper, is silver trimming
As the customer may desire.

A touch of glamour to the costume
Are pins and earrings too,
Enameled in bright rainbow colors
A choice that one would never rue.

There are other added features
To this ever growing stock,
Felt accessories with sparkling sequins
Brighten up the plainest frock.

There are book marks that are useful
For the one who cares to read,
And a novel case for glasses
Apt to be lost when most in need.

Attractive little Balsam pillows
Bring the Woodlands to the mind,
Spicy odors fresh and fragrant
A pleasing gift as one could find.

There is even home-made candy
Peanut-brittle, fudge or butter-scotch,
For the ones who are not conscious
That their waist-lines they should watch.

The Old Feed Mill has more to offer
Than the gifts that are on display,
Flowers of various shades or colors
Add their beauty in bright array.

Landscapes and flowers were often featured in Grace's work, and pictures such as these now decorate many homes in the area.

It might well be called a Rose Garden
For Roses are a specialty,
And the fragrant flower-petals
Make a marvelous potpourri.

To the partner goes all honors
For the Herb-bed so ably planned,
Sage and marjoram, thyme and parsley
Thrive under her efficient hand.

Lively little yellow kittens
Roll and tumble in their play,
And delight the younger children
In a most amusing way.

Though the lively stream of water
That still flows behind the Mill,
Cannot be of former service
Fishermen test their angling skill.

So while passing through this valley
Though the grinders now are still,
One may yet renew fond memories
By calling at The Old Feed Mill.

Elizabeth C. Jones
July 1956

Several years before Grace died she sold the home and the mill, but retained the privilege of living in the house the remainder of her life. She was so thankful that she was able to stay in her own home where she could still hear the sound of the brook through her windows and enjoy the beautiful scenery around her—the countryside where she spent her childhood and that she so dearly loved.

Recently the old mill has been named to the National Register of Historic Sites. It has changed hands again since Miss Paull sold the mill and the house to Ray Smith. After her death, Ray sold the property to a Mr. McGhee who intends to restore the mill.

Charcoal drawing of Gordon Paull, as he appeared in several cowboy stories.

5. *Community Activities*

Grace loved little children and they loved her too. Many times she would come to the Poland Public Library in the summertime at their story hour. She would draw charcoal pictures of animals and people as she told a story. These she would give to the children to take home.

A newspaper article published in the *Utica Observer-Dispatch* November 29, 1968, by Lyn Simon tells about a cat and a dog that Miss Paull owned:

> Once upon a time, as all good children's tales begin, there lived a lady, a cat, and a dog in a big yellow house by an Old Mill.
>
> The cat, severely independent and impeccably clean, was named "Chippie." The dog, noisily gregarious, and with the habit of greeting people from the rooftop of the house, was named "Patsy." The lady was . . . and is . . . Grace Paull, illustrator and author of children's books, who has spent much of her life in the never-never land of Children's Dreams.

Grace and her sister Sara were both active members of Cold Brook United Methodist Church. They taught Sunday School classes and participated in fund-raising projects for many years. During the time Miss Paull operated the Old Feed Mill Gallery, she invited the church to hold their summer fund-raising project, the Koffee Klatch, there. It was always a delightful occasion and a financial success.

When the Cold Brook United Methodist Church celebrated its 150th Anniversary in 1979, a book was written on the history of the church stating the names of the ministers and presiding elders and church families. On the cover of the book is the lithograph of the church which Grace Paull had made in the 1940s.

Grace and her sister Sara also affiliated with the Community Baptist Church in Poland, where they also taught Sunday School classes and belonged to the Dorcas Circle.

Knowing that Henry Blue, for years, was a newspaper reporter and photographer for both the *Utica Observer-Dispatch* and the *Herkimer Evening Telegram,* my daughter and I spent a Saturday morning looking through his well-kept scrapbooks. I came across an article that I had been searching for. Winifred had told me that her aunt went to Russia with another lady when she was seventy-five years old. Winifred didn't remember much about it, only that she remembered her aunt saying that they served them carrots for every meal. Here is a more accurate report as found in Henry's scrapbook. The article is marked with the date January 1975.

> Miss Grace Paull of Cold Brook, well-known illustrator and author of children's books and owner of the Cold Brook Feed Mill Gallery, and Miss Marcia Smith, librarian of the Adirondack Museum at Blue Mountain Lake, study maps of a trip they will take next month to Russia. They will visit museums and art centers in Moscow, Leningrad, and Kalinin. It will be Miss Paull's first trip abroad. Miss Smith, a former librarian at Herkimer High School, has made several trips to foreign countries in past years. They will leave February 10 and return 10 days later.

Grace and her good friend Ethel Swantees were both very much interested in community affairs and took part in the activities around them. In 1976, when the village of Cold Brook celebrated its Bicentennial, a book was published telling many stories about the settlement of Cold Brook and its original families.

Artwork for the Cold Brook Bicentennial Book.

Ethel and Grace contributed a great deal of their time to the Cold Brook Bicentennial Committee in organizing the book for publication. Grace drew the frontispiece, using the historic objects produced in factories operated by the water power of Cold Brook as motifs in her border designs, while Ethel researched some of the historical facts about those industries.

Grace Paull with two of Poland's Retired Teachers, Alida Lanning and Evelyn Tudhope, at Dorothy Buck's home.

Miss Paull taught art one year in the elementary grades in the Barneveld and Poland Central Schools and she belonged to the Poland Retired Teachers Organization, as do I. She loved to attend our monthly luncheons to be with her many friends and to enjoy eating out. She had a saying: "Some people eat to live, but I live to eat!" Grace had a kind word for everyone and always appreciated what others did for her. Oftentimes when she came to our meetings, she would say, "Isn't it nice to be with friends?"

During the last few year of her life, Grace suffered severely from arthritis. It had crippled her to the point where she needed two canes in order to walk. She had a chair lift installed in her home. Her eyesight was failing her, but she kept her sense of humor—she was full of fun, always smiling, and good-natured.

Another one of Miss Paull's sayings, quite often repeated was: "Yard by yard, life is hard; inch by inch, life's a cinch!" Truly, considering all the things that she accomplished during a lifetime, one cannot help but think that she lived her life inch by inch.

She remained active in the community and lived in the old yellow house by the mill until she died August 17, 1990, at the age of 91.

6. Nieces and Nephews

The old farmhouse still stands on Cold Brook Hill. It has gone through many changes over the years. Paul and Marjorie Frazier bought the property in 1987 and moved into the home two years later. Paul has retired from Munson-Williams-Proctor Institute where he taught art and sculpting for several years. Marjorie is a therapist in New Hartford. She also practices from her home in Cold Brook.

Looking out their window, they have a view of the beautiful home owned by the Arvin Trevvett family. Arvin added rooms onto Grace Paull's studio several years ago, and it became their residence. For years at Christmas time the Trevvetts placed a big tree in the window of the studio portion of the house. It was a sight to behold!

Arvin and his wife have passed away, but two of their sons, John and William, still live there. Edward is married and lives in Canandaigua, New York, and David lives near Elmira, New York.

James Trevvett and his family live next door. They have a daughter, Amy, and a son, James II.

The Trevvett home in Poland, New York.

Winifred Trevvett Hall lives nearby. She has three daughters—Sandra, Ann, and Christine—and a son Irving (Skip). Her daughters and their families live in the area also. Skip's family live at Nelson, New York.

Herbert and Doris Trevvett live in Poland. Herbert is the Chief Executive Officer of Commercial Travelers, an insurance company in Utica formerly owned by his father, Edward Trevvett. James Trevvett also works for the insurance company.

Grace's notepaper depicted such familiar winter scenes as children sledding and Poland's village center.

Doris is active in the Community Baptist Church of Poland, where her father preached for several years. She is the choir director, past trustee, and also a member of the M & M Women's Group. Doris and Herbert have three children—Paul, Tom, and Debbie.

Gordon Paull lives in Herkimer. His mother and father, Jennie and Theodore, always ran the farm. Gordon still is in the farming business. He works for the Dairy Herd Improvement Co-op, keeping business management records for farmers.

Elsie Paull married James Wilcott. They lived several places during their marriage, including Washington, D.C.; Virginia; Tokyo, Japan; and finally settled at Concord, California. Elsie died a few years ago and James still lives at Concord. Their son, Steven, lives in San Francisco.

7. Recognitions and Memories

On September 12, 1973, the Mid-York Library System, a distributing library in Utica, held a workshop featuring Grace Paull and her work. The following is a transcription of the speech given by Miss Ruth Auert on that occasion:

> I think it was a phrase of a little fourth-grader who came to the Institute [Munson-Williams-Proctor], to be toured through Fountain Elms and the Art Museum, who wrote subsequently a letter to Mrs. Zogby, our leader, and said, "Dear Miss Auert, I don't know how a lady like you could know so much about art."
>
> I don't know how Mr. Hasemeier could know so much about me. The hat situation makes me want to mention a hat that I had, Grace, when you and I were attending a luncheon given by Mr. Grant some years ago. An autographing party followed, and it was a brown hat and had a feather shaped like a question mark, and somebody said, "How did it happen that you chose that?" I couldn't think of anything to say, but since then I have thought probably I was always in quite a state of uncertainty. And,

believe it or not, subsequently to that, at a bank conclave, I had another hat with a question mark, and so there must be something about it. . . .

I am the devoted slave of *all* librarians, which makes me a friend to you. I couldn't do without the public library; the reference room sees me there frequently. I am always on the telephone. I have asked all sorts of questions,

Grace Paull and Ruth Auert look over a collection of Miss Paull's books displayed for the Mid-York Library System Workshop held in September 1973.

sensible and non-sensible, and I see some smiling faces who would bear this out and know from experience. Because I was involved in a fashion show as commentator, I even had the librarians doing research on fig leaves.

If asked to nominate a site for landmark preservation, I shall suggest the old flour mill, the 1858 grist mill in Cold Brook, New York. Route-wise it is on #8 about 18 miles from Utica. En route to Piseco Lake in the North Country, the traveler will wisely proceed slowly not to miss the picturesque mill with the winding, willful brook and its waterwheel in the background. Cold Brook is the kind of stream that never made up its mind which side of the road to stay on, so it crosses the road again and again impartially.

It is worth a stop to browse among the shop's wares—the candles, the imports and the local crafts, basketry, pottery, gourmet foods, gifts from all nations. Here you will see watercolors and lithographs, and most likely you will meet the proprietor of the shop and gallery, Grace Paull, author and illustrator of children's books. If she isn't in the mill, she'll be in her yellow house next door and will come out to welcome you.

Miss Paull was born in upstate New York, a daughter of the late Mr. and Mrs. A. R. Paull.

Her father's work in the paper mill business caused the family to move about, and Grace spent her childhood there and in New Hampshire and Montreal, Canada. She attended Utica Free Academy where her ability was recognized and encouraged by the Art Supervisor, Miss Mabel Northrup. Later she attended Pratt Institute, Grand Central Art School, and the Art Students' League in New York City. She pays tribute, always, to those who furthered her art training: Alexander Archipenko, George Bridgman, Alan Lewis, and to George C. Miller, the lithographer.

To satisfy a desire for more original color work, she was enrolled in an art class at Munson-Williams-Proctor Institute. After many years of wintering in New York, she is now permanently settled in her house in Cold Brook village. She has said,

> And what a comfortable feeling it is, knowing that come fall, I will not have to pack up my reference books and my pencils and go hunting for a reasonable room or two in which to live and work through the winter months. I still do a lithograph occasionally. I go to New York once or twice a year and am always delighted to return to my cat, my dog, and all out-of-doors to look at from my window. And gardening still remains a special hobby.

The Cold Brook Methodist Church was chosen by the American Artists' Group for use as a Christmas card.

It was the well-known Norcross Company that interested Miss Paull in designing greeting cards—among them recalled yesterday, a valentine with the message "Next to myself, I like you best." Her Christmas card designs have been used by the American Artists' Group of New York, her prints have been exhibited at the Corcoran Gallery in New York, the Philadelphia Print Show, the National Academy in New York, and at the Munson-Williams-Proctor Institute.

Modestly, she has accepted honors. Graciously, she acknowledges the helpfulness of others. She illustrated Carolyn Bailey's *Pioneer Art in America* and gave credit. Acknowledgement is made to five museums "for the very real and generous assistance given in my search for reference material which would make these illustrations historically accurate." This denotes the measurement of a great, but humble person. Many distinctions have come to her. The Pennell Funds for the Library of Congress purchased one of her lithographs, and she received a First Purchase Award at Laguna Beach, California.

But it is as author and illustrator of children's books and books for young people in the teens that she is best known and best loved.

In 1932, she illustrated a book by Marjorie Bianco, *Street of Little Shops.* From then on her stories and her drawings were sought by the great publishing houses: Doubleday, Viking Press, Crowell, Stokes, and Macmillan.

Grace and her young friend Nancy Coonradt provided the models for the characters in *A Squash for the Fair*, published in 1943 by Doubleday, Doran.

Our author has said that it has been her extra-school, out-of-doors activities that have been most influential in determining her choice of her profession. There was mountain climbing in New Hampshire, skating and skiing and show-shoeing in Canada, roaming the fields and woods, following the trout streams, sketching the animals and the country mill on the farm in New York State. A life-long fondness for all these things combined with an equal fondness for books—what else could she do but make books for boys and girls who love all these activities too? And so we have *Peanut Butter's Slide, A Squash for the Fair, They Had a Blue Cart, Raspberry Patch,* and *Pancakes for Breakfast,* to mention some of my favorites, and many others.

Answering the need for an elementary grade teacher of art in Barneveld and Poland, Miss Paull says of this experience, "I suppose it's good source material, but it's hard work too. I've had to give up my own drawing temporarily to spend all my time preparing for school. It's very strenuous." She adds, "I've always worked by myself, and getting other people to do the work is hard." Those of us who have been teachers know what she means.

Author Grace Paull understands and loves children. Niece Winifred, sister Sara's daughter, is the star of *Raspberry Patch,* and I always thought I recognized her brothers as characters in others of her books—that would be Arvin and Herbert and Jim. You see, I was once those children's Sunday School teacher.

Her nieces and nephews admire their accomplished "Aunt Grace." Besides this, they like her, remembering the birthday parties she arranged for them and the Palomino she cared for and let them ride. Now there is a succession of grand-nieces and grand-nephews.

Grace, do you remember the luncheon arranged by Lambert Grant, son of John L. Grant? I speak of this because some of us have lived in Utica long enough to remember the book shop which was on the site of the East-West Arterial in the vicinity of the old "hump" over which the trolley cars passed—the elevated bridge over the Erie Canal. Grant's Book Store was your first employer, or one of the first, I believe. You were guest of honor at that occasion and autographed our books.

Among the wild flowers around the porch of the old mill is a wrought-iron marker which bears this ageless verse: "The kiss of the sun for pardon, The song of the birds for mirth, One is nearer God's heart in a garden, Than anywhere else on earth." I always look for the marker where the Brown-Eyed Susans, the wild asters, the goldenrod, and the Queen

> Anne's Lace grow. It speaks to me of Grace Paull, of her contribution to the pleasure of children and of those not too old to be children. It isn't for sale, but there's no charge if you wish to memorize it. Thank you.

In 1979, Grace Paull was one of eight area artists honored with a show at Utica's Munson-Williams-Proctor Institute's presentation of Realists of Central New York.

A year or so before Grace died, a dedication ceremony was held at the Poland Central School. One section of the children's library is filled with the books she wrote and illustrated.

The Mid-York Library System had many of her children's books in their collection. After Miss Paull died, they gave the entire collection to the Poland Public Library. These books have been out of print for a long time, but they are still being read and enjoyed by the children in this area. A complete list of the books given to the library is contained in the Appendix.

After her death in 1990, the Poland Retired Teachers had one of Grace's watercolors of her studio framed by Al Casatelli to hang in the children's section of the Poland Public Library. Librarian Paula Johnson accepted the painting from the group's president, Marian Jones.

Munson-Williams-Proctor Institute, where her work has been shown many times, bought her "October's Bright Blue Weather" for its permanent collection. Her prints were also exhibited in the St. John's Art Galleries, Village Art Center, Greenwich Village, New York.

Having known that Frances Warren, librarian at Poland Central School for many years, was a very special friend of Grace's, I asked her to reflect on her friendship with her. These are her memories of Grace:

> Grace . . . is so clear in my mind. I'll try to put those thoughts down in writing. It does us good to think deeply about folks who have mattered to us.
>
> I was one of the fortunate ones to become a close friend of Grace Paull's. I was there to share her thinking when she first built the studio on the hill. I enjoyed so very much learning about her close relationship with Helen Sewell, the illustrator of children's books. They worked very closely together, may even have shared an apartment together. Their work was similar. I think they had both been employed to do greeting cards which Grace found excellent training for detail. About then Grace's list of books she had illustrated was growing.

Grace, Herbie Trevvett, and Kenneth McVoy were models for *A Horse to Ride*, published by Doubleday in 1949.

Soon she was putting out her own stories for which she used our local children as models. I was so happy to have my nephew, Bill Holliday, as one of the children on horseback in *A Horse to Ride.* I think *Pancakes for Breakfast* was the very favorite of the children in the Poland Central School. Having something done on the maple syrup that is so special in the area had great meaning.

It wasn't until Grace had moved to the old mill that I found her coming to our library club at school. She accepted the title of Honorary Member, took time to come to judge our elaborate Book Week exhibits, and invited us to her home for desserts. I recall once that inquisitive fingers broke a lovely porcelain from Italy. She was careful not to let the student feel badly. All those occasions were demanding of her time, but she never showed reluctance to respond to our invitations.

I enjoyed knowing her sister Sara, who came with her to my camp at Piseco. At one of those visits Grace painted a lovely picture of my lake front which she gave to me as a gift, together with a frame. It now resides with Bill Holliday, who was happy to protect it for me when I moved West. Because it meant so much to him, I didn't want to ask for it back but ordered a new one. My home was not complete without Grace's vision of my lake home. She glorified it for me.

I spent a lot of time in the mill, sharing her special delights, and enjoying the history it restored.

Grace's nephews Gordon and Arvin were the models for *Peanut Butter's Slide*, published by Viking Press in 1939.

Appendix

Grace Paull's Books from the Mid-York Library System given to the Poland Public Library

Books Written and Illustrated by Grace Paull

Cement Work for Sport and Skinny	Viking Press	1940
Come to the City	Abelard-Schuman	1959
Come to the Country	Abelard-Schuman	1956
Four Friends	Grosset & Dunlap	1935
Freddy the Curious Cat	Doubleday	1958
Gloomy the Camel	Viking Press	1938
A Horse to Ride	Doubleday	1949
A Little Twin	Doubleday	1953
Pancakes for Breakfast	Doubleday	1946
Peanut Butter's Slide	Viking Press	1939
Raspberry Patch	Doubleday	1941
Snowed-in Hill	Abelard Press	1953
Some Day	Abelard-Schuman	1957
A Squash for the Fair	Doubleday, Doran	1943
They Had a Blue Cart	Whitman	1935

Books Illustrated by Grace Paull

Title / Author	Publisher	Year
Adventure in Courage: The Story of Theodore Roosevelt by Frances Cavanah	Rand McNally	1961
Augustus by Claire Huchet Bishop	Viking Press	1945
Benjie's Hat by Mabel Leigh Hunt	Frederick Stokes	1937
Betsy and the Proud House by Mary Urmston	Doubleday	1947
Betsy Ross and the Flag by Jane Mayer	Random House	1947
The Bounces of Cynthiann by Evelyn Sibley Lampman	Doubleday	1950
Carry On, Grumms! by Bessie F. White	Ariel Books	1956
Children of the Handcrafts by Carolyn Sherwin Bailey	Viking Press	1952
Country-Stop by Carolyn Sherwin Bailey	Viking Press	1942
Crazy Creek by Evelyn Sibley Lampman	Doubleday	1948
Dancing Tom by Elizabeth Coatsworth	Macmillan	1938
Dody and Cap-Tin Jinks by Helen Ferris	Doubleday	1939
Downstreet with Edith by Hildreth T. Wriston	Doubleday, Doran	1935
A Feather Bed for Toby Tod by Katherine Reeves	Crowell	1959
The First Year by Enid L. Meadowcroft	Crowell	1937
Forgotten Island by Elizabeth Coatsworth	Grosset & Dunlap	1942
The Good Friends by Margery Bianco	Viking Press	1934

Illustration for Carolyn Sherwin Bailey's *Country-Stop*, published in 1952 by Viking Press.

Green Grows the Garden by Margery Bianco	Macmillan	1936
Heydays and Holidays by Laura Harris	Garden City Publishers	1945
Homespun Playdays by Carolyn Sherwin Bailey	Viking Press	1941
Jean and Company Unlimited by Helen Perry Curtis	John C. Winston	1937
Jesus the Children's Friend by Mary Edna Lloyd	Abingdon Press	1955
Jesus the Little New Baby by Mary Edna Lloyd	Abingdon-Cokesbury	1951
Jo's Boys by Louisa May Alcott	World	1957
Katie Meets Buffalo Bill by Katharine Koch	Grosset & Dunlap	1945
Lending Mary by Eliza Orne White	Houghton Mifflin	1934
The Little Girl with Seven Names by Mabel Leigh Hunt	Frederick Stokes	1936
The Little Haymakers by Elizabeth Coatsworth	Macmillan	1949
Liz'Beth Ann's Goat by Mary Virginia Provines	Viking Press	1947
Lulu Herself by Elisabeth H. Lansing	Crowell	1956
Lulu's Window by Elisabeth H. Lansing	Crowell	1954
The Middle Sister by Miriam E. Mason	Macmillan	1947
Mystery of the Old Barn by Mary Urmston	Doubleday	1945
Peter by the Sea by Julian R. Meade	Doubleday, Doran	1940
Pioneer Art in America by Carolyn Sherwin Bailey	Viking Press	1944

Polly Poppingay Milliner by Gertrude Newman	Lippincott	1943
The Purple Giant with the Pink Toe Nails by William C. White & William I. White	Aldus Printers	1956
A Ranch for Danny by Clyde Robert Bulla	Crowell	1951
Riding the Pony Express by Clyde Robert Bulla	Crowell	1948
Rowena Carey by Ruth Holberg	Doubleday	1949
Rowena the Sailor by Ruth Langland Holberg	Doubleday	1954
Sandy's Spurs by Lavinia R. Davis	Doubleday	1951
The Secret Valley by Clyde Robert Bulla	Crowell	1949
The Seven and Sam by Mary Urmston	Doubleday	1955
The Silver Spoon Mystery by Dorothy Sterling	Doubleday	1958
A Star for Hansi by Marguerite Vance	Harper Brothers	1936
Star of Wild Horse Canyon by Clyde Robert Bulla	Crowell	1953
Story Parade Green Book: A Collection of Modern Stories for Boys and Girls	John C. Winston	1938
Story Parade Rainbow Book: A Collection of Modern Stories for Boys and Girls	John C. Winston	1942
Story Parade Star Book: A Collection of Modern Stories for Boys and Girls	John C. Winston	1944
A Street of Little Shops by Margery Williams Bianco	Doubleday, Doran	1932

Bob and Susan McVoy with one of his vintage cars, an illustration from *Teeny and the Tall Man,* published by Doubleday, Doran in 1936.

Surprise for a Cowboy by Clyde Robert Bulla	Crowell	1950
Swamp Shack Mystery by Mary Urmston	Doubleday	1959
Teeny and the Tall Man by Julian R. Meade	Doubleday, Doran	1936
Tomboy Row by Ruth Langland Holberg	Doubleday	1952
Tops and Whistles by Carolyn Sherwin Bailey	Viking Press	1937
Trudy the Motherly Hen by Elizabeth S. Helfman	Messner	1954
Uncle Sam's Story Book by Wilhelmina Harper	David McKay	1944
The Wabash Knows the Secret by Elisabeth H. Friermood	Doubleday	1951
Winter on the Prairie by Alice B. Curtis	Crowell	1945
The Wonderful Baker by Mabel Leigh Hunt	Lippincott	1950

Synopses of selected books written and illustrated by Grace Paull taken from book jackets

Come to the Country
Abelard-Schuman, 1956

This book contains full-page pictures of many things that can be seen in the country. There is a small caption on each page and the pictures tell the whole story.

Gloomy the Camel
Viking Press, 1938

There is probably nothing more sorrowful looking than a sad camel, and Gloomy was very sad. He lived a comfortable life in a nice zoo, but he felt that he wasn't useful, which made him feel very low in his mind.

Janey and her mother found Gloomy gloomy when they visited the zoo, and this is how they changed his frame of mind and his nickname.

A Horse to Ride
Doubleday, 1949

A Horse to Ride is about a little boy who loves horses and a Palomino who loves little boys in the country.

The story begins when Terry who wanted a horse to ride and Aunt Mary who wanted a horse to ride first met Turk. Turk was a golden colored horse with a white mane and a white tail. All through the summer Turk was a very nice horse to ride, but when fall came Terry and his Aunt Mary had to find a place for Turk to live. Turk helps them find his winter home.

A Little Twin

Doubleday, 1953

Tommy had a problem. He wanted one of Rhoda's twin calves for his own. Big Brother Benny had Big Twin to groom and train for the 4-H Fair in the fall. But Tommy was too little to belong to the 4-H—too little, they said, to take care of Little Twin himself.

Tommy didn't agree. He knew he could do whatever Benny did. All summer he was Benny's shadow. Whatever Benny did for Big Twin, he did for Little Twin. When September and Fair Day rolled around, it was Benny and Big Twin who had the problem.

And Tommy and Little Twin had an unexpected adventure.

Pancakes for Breakfast

Doubleday, 1946

A rousing winter holiday with Ann and Peter on an upstate New York farm, with skiing and sleigh rides, trips to the sugar bush and all kinds of winter farm fun.

(Breakfast, of course, is pancakes and homemade maple syrup).

Peanut Butter's Slide
Viking Press, 1939

The story of Sports McAllister and his cousin Skinny McAllister and their goat Peanut Butter McAllister is told as much in pictures as in words. You'll like both.

The fact is, the goat and the two boys were always together when the boys weren't in school. One thing they always liked to do was slide. They slid down everything, and sometimes it wasn't so comfortable. And then one day Father Bill came home with a new car and the back of it made a perfect slide. Father Bill didn't like the idea much, so he bought them a real honest-to-goodness slide, which they used all the time.

Raspberry Patch
Doubleday, 1941

When Mary Jane goes with her mother to pick raspberries for jam, she discovers a lot of things in the raspberry patch besides berries.

A Squash for the Fair
Doubleday, Doran, 1943

Mary Jane's first garden and what happens to her squash at the School Fair makes an engaging picture book.